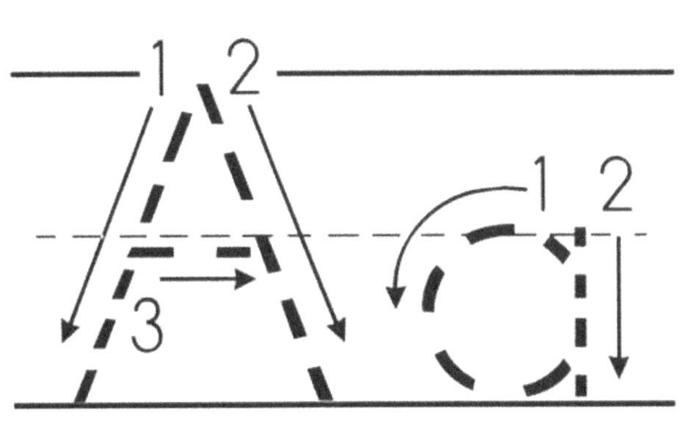

TRACE THE LETTERS AND WRITE
YOUR OWN ON THE REMAINING LINE

A A A A A A A

A A A A A A A

A A A A A A A

A A A A A A A

A A A A A A A

A A A A A A A

Trace the letters and write your own on the remaining line.

B B B B B B

B B B B B B

B B B B B B

B B B B B B

B B B B B B

B B B B B B

b b b b b b b

b b b b b b b

b b b b b b b

b b b b b b b

b b b b b b b

b b b b b b b

Trace the letters and write your own on the remaining line.

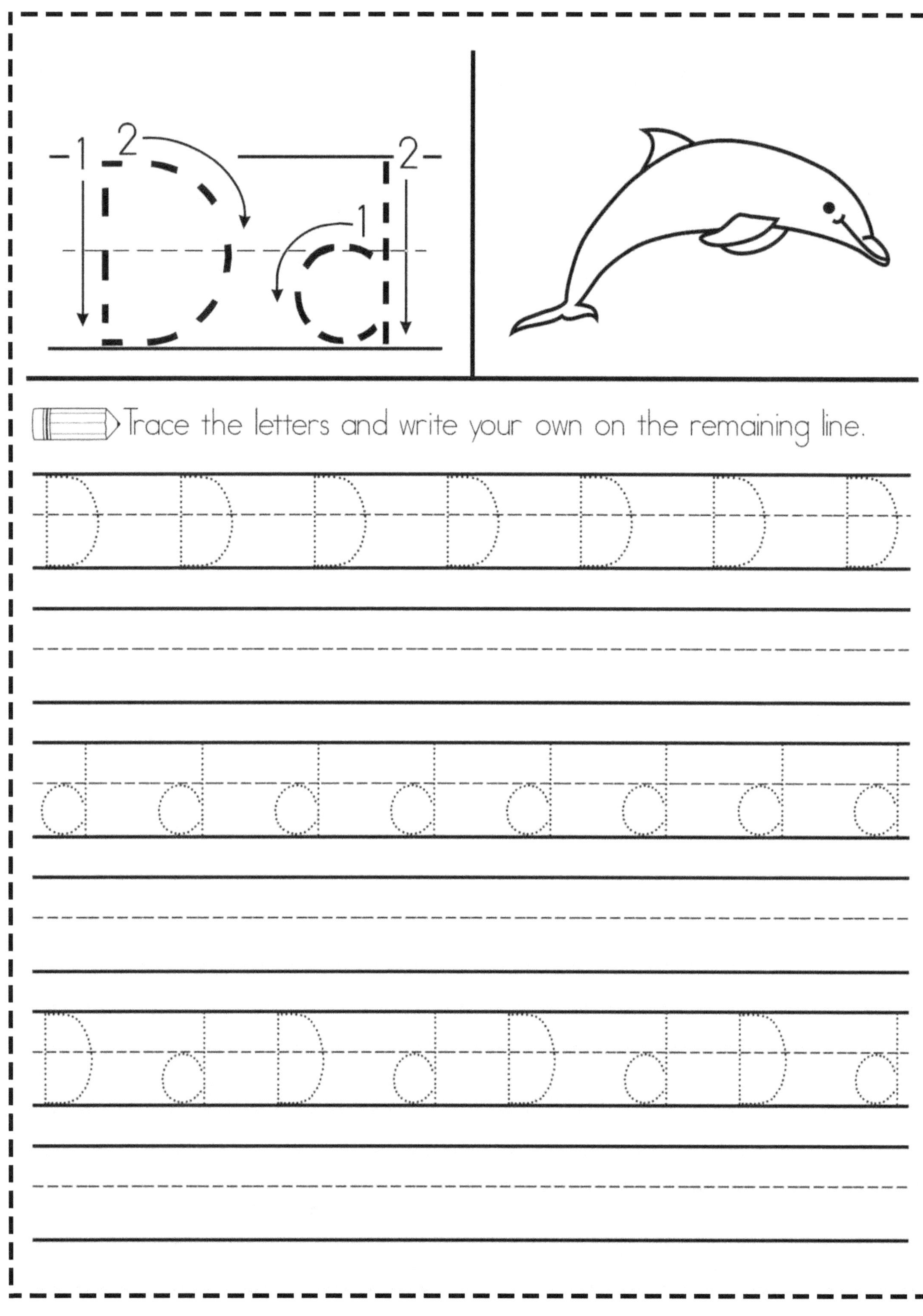

Trace the letters and write your own on the remaining line.

Trace the letters and write your own on the remaining line.

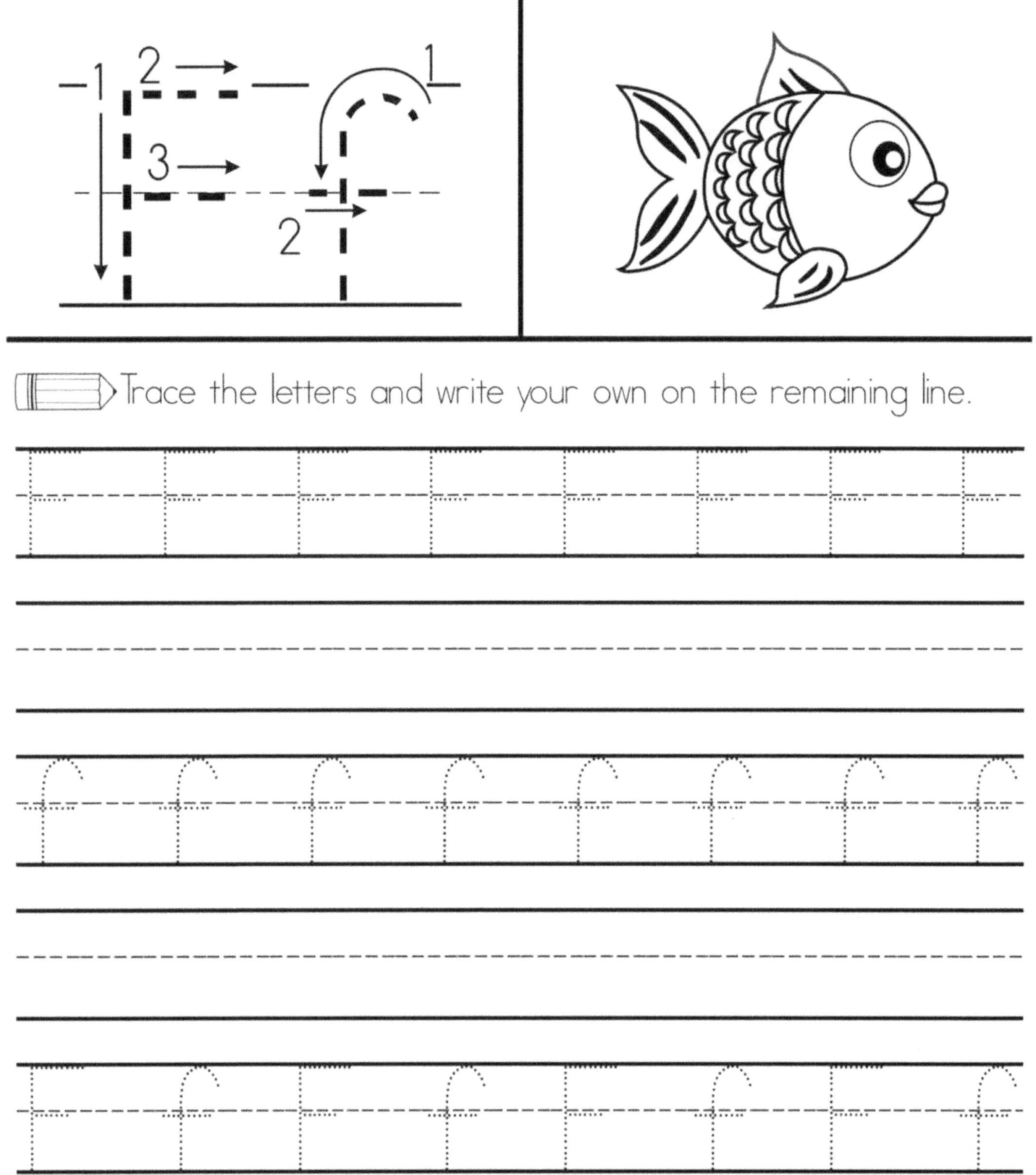

✏️ Trace the letters and write your own on the remaining line.

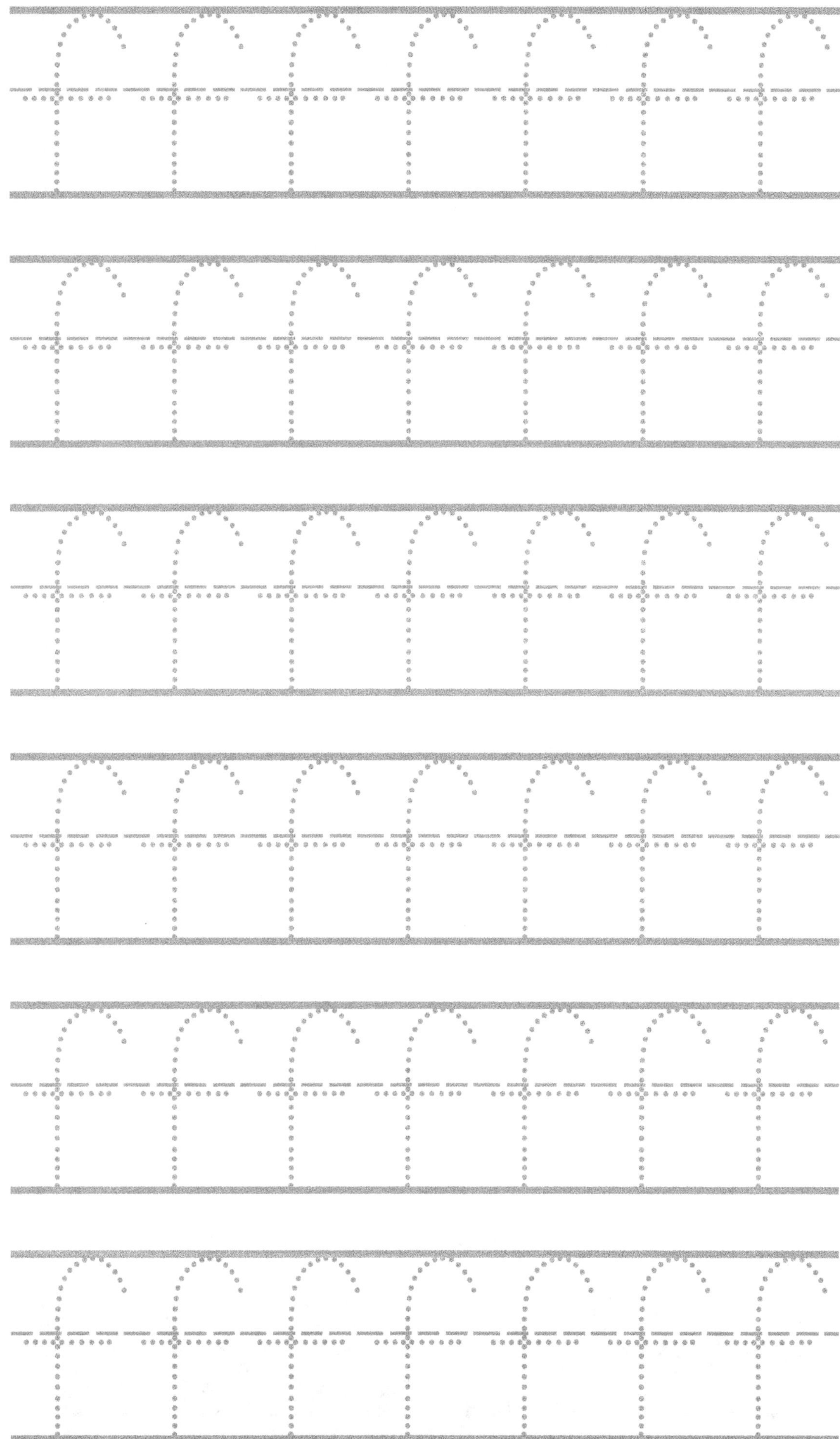

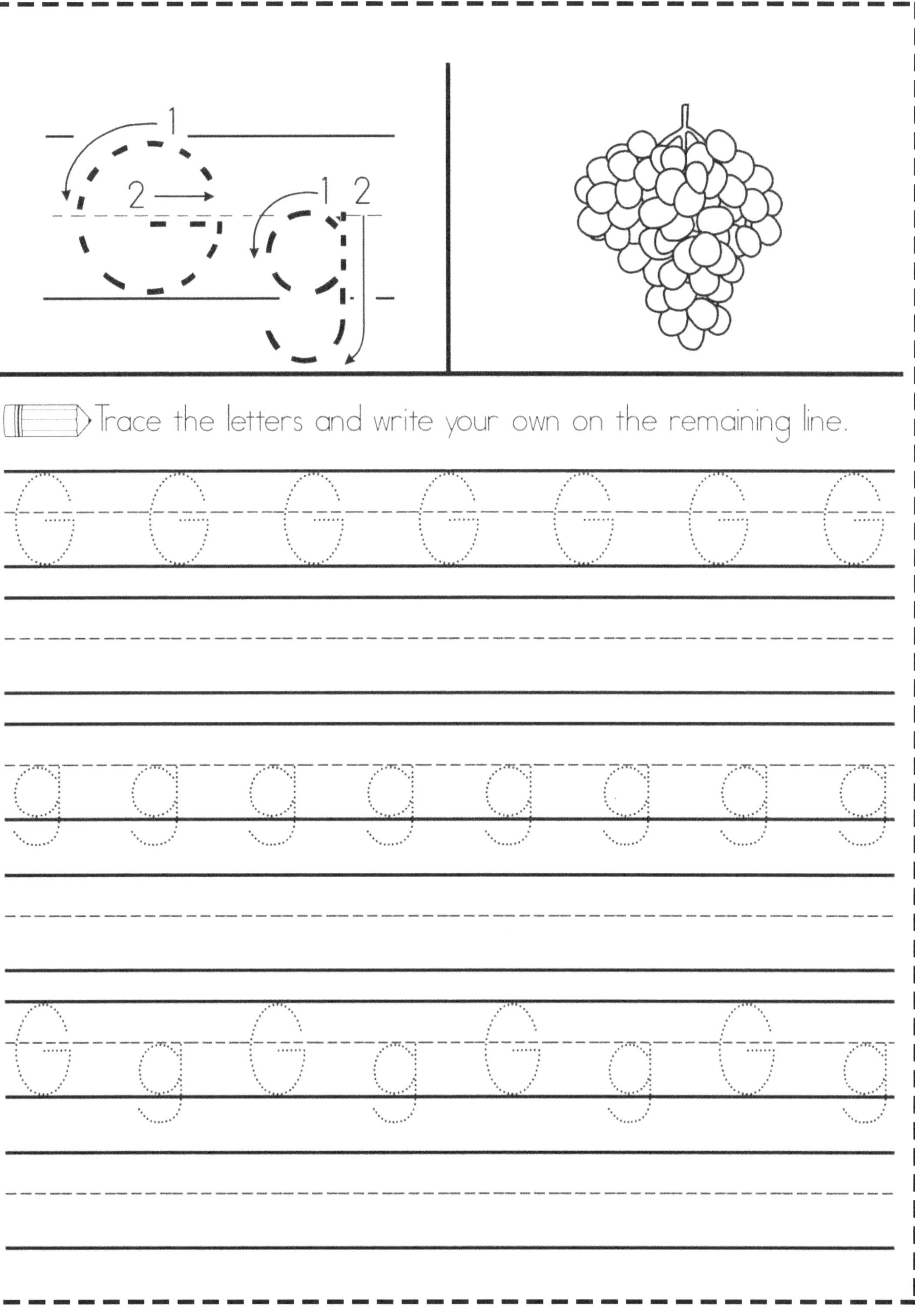

Trace the letters and write your own on the remaining line.

G G G G G G G

G G G G G G G

G G G G G G G

G G G G G G G

G G G G G G G

G G G G G G G

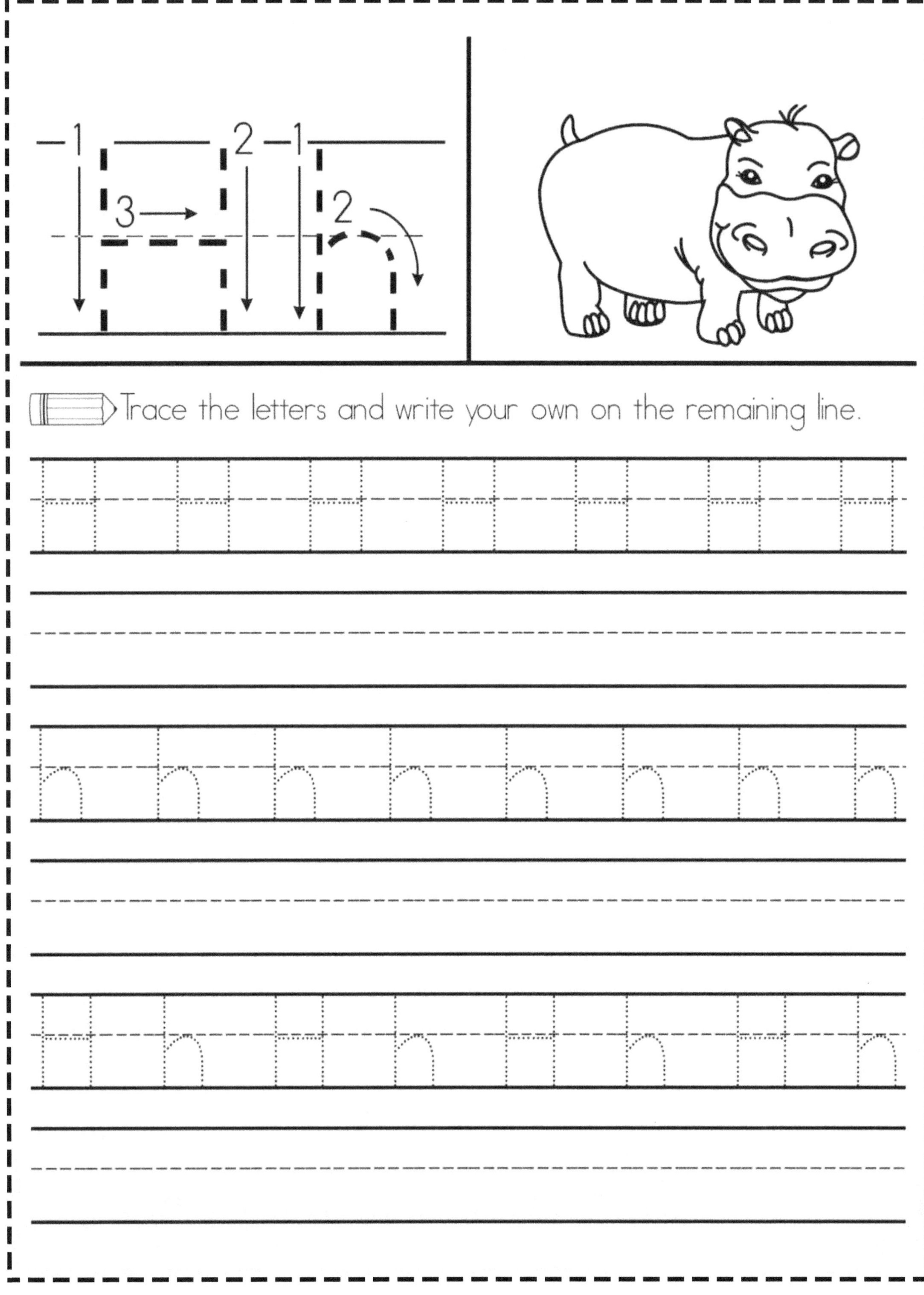

Trace the letters and write your own on the remaining line.

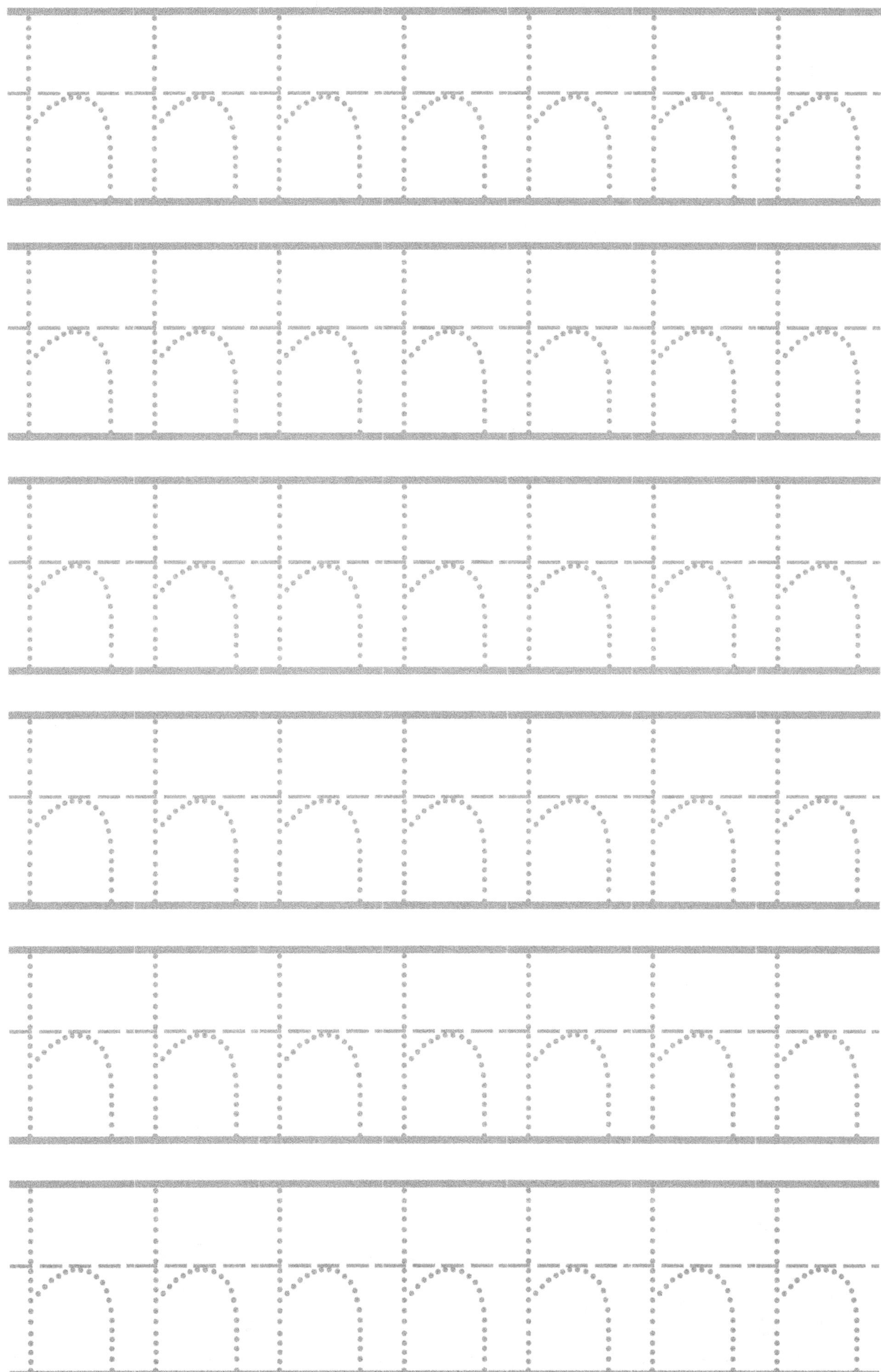

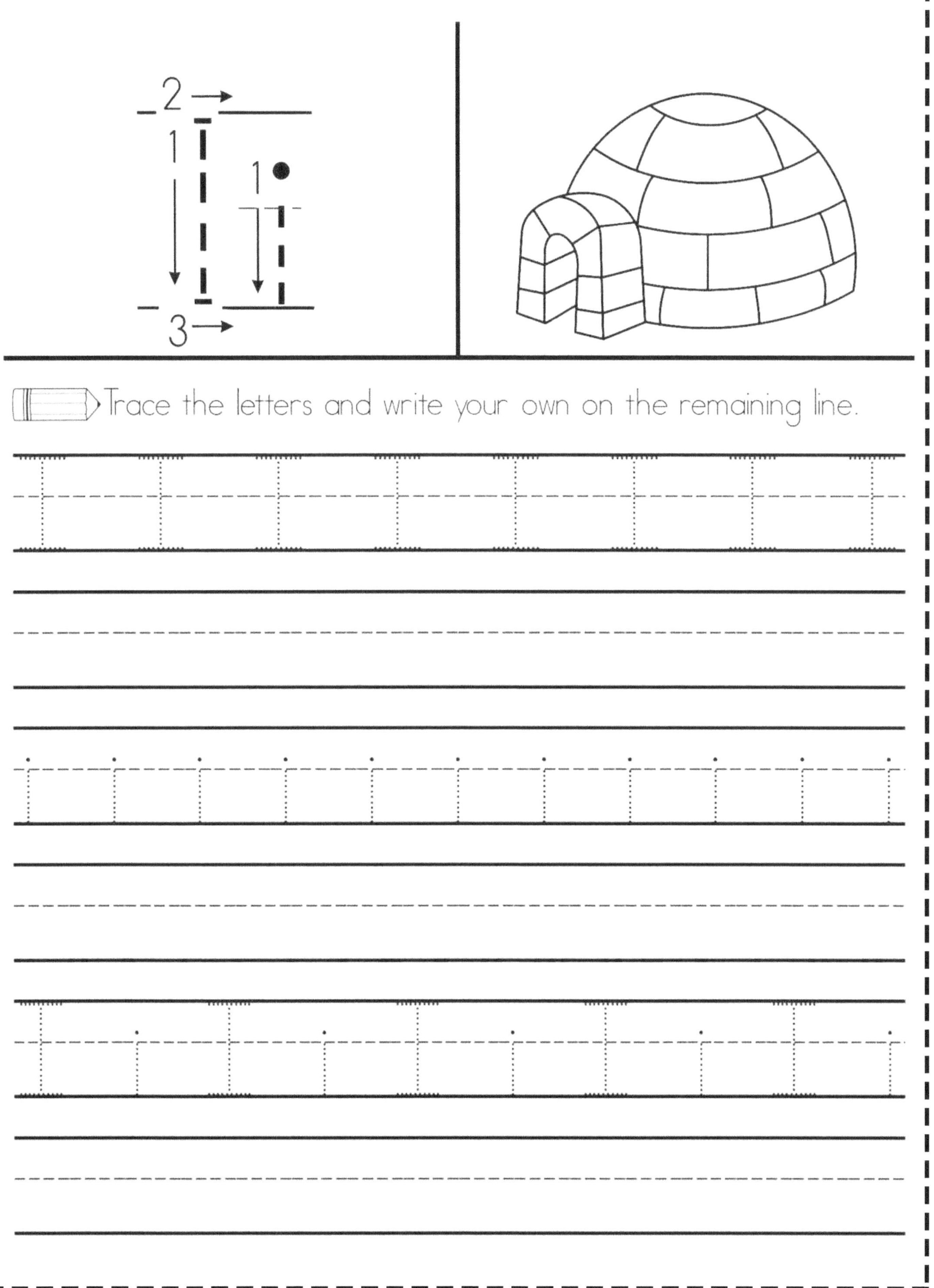

Trace the letters and write your own on the remaining line.

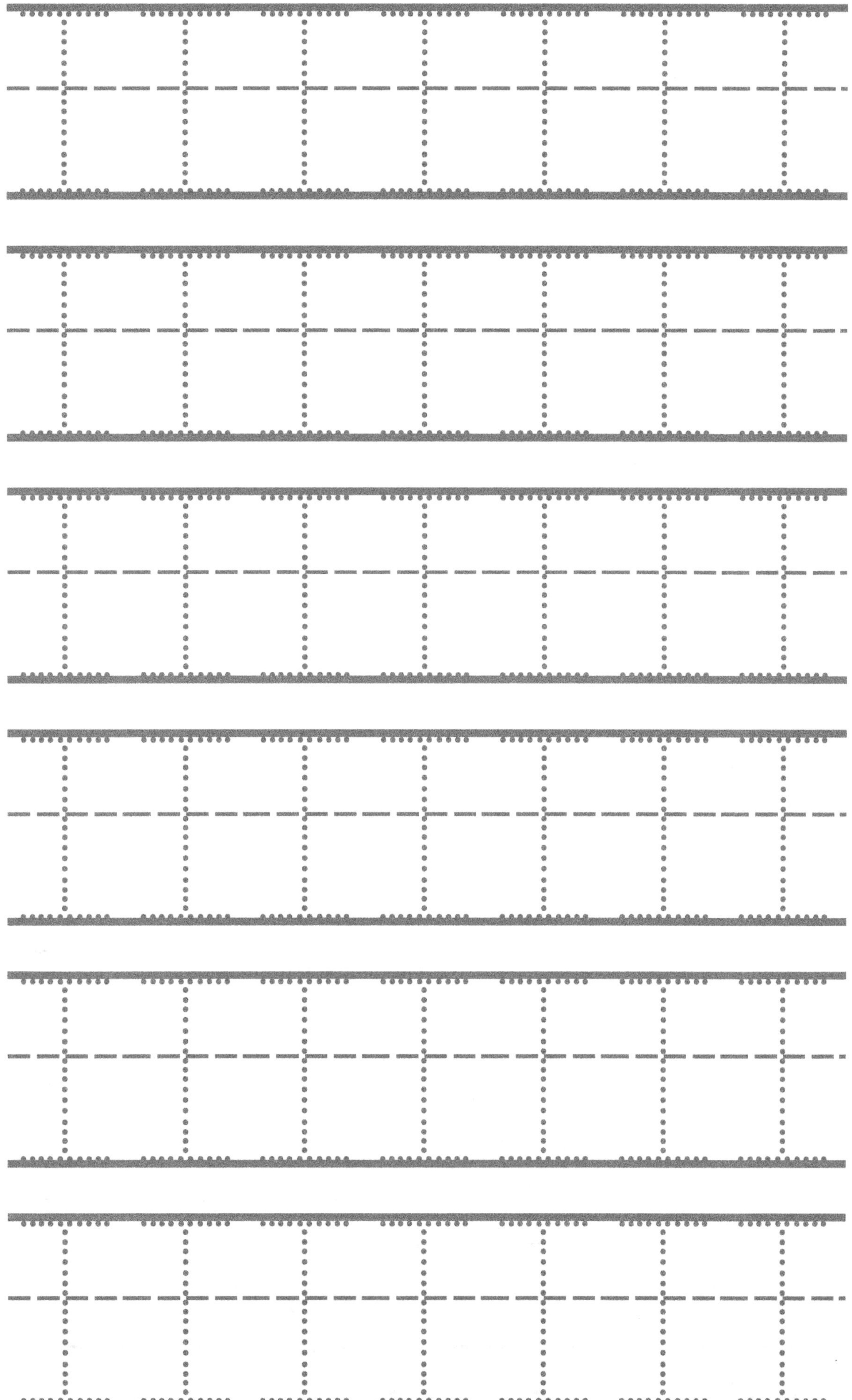

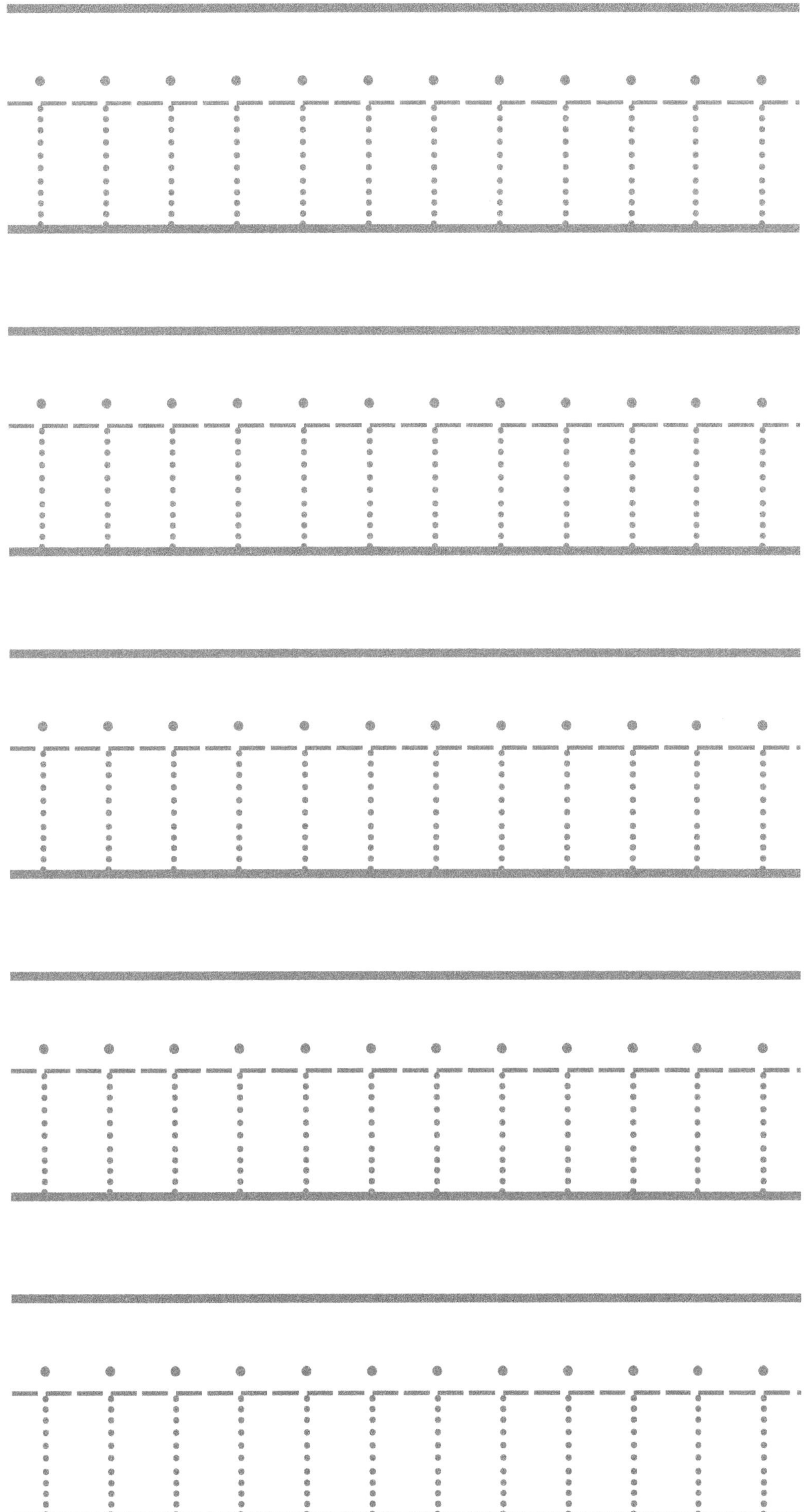

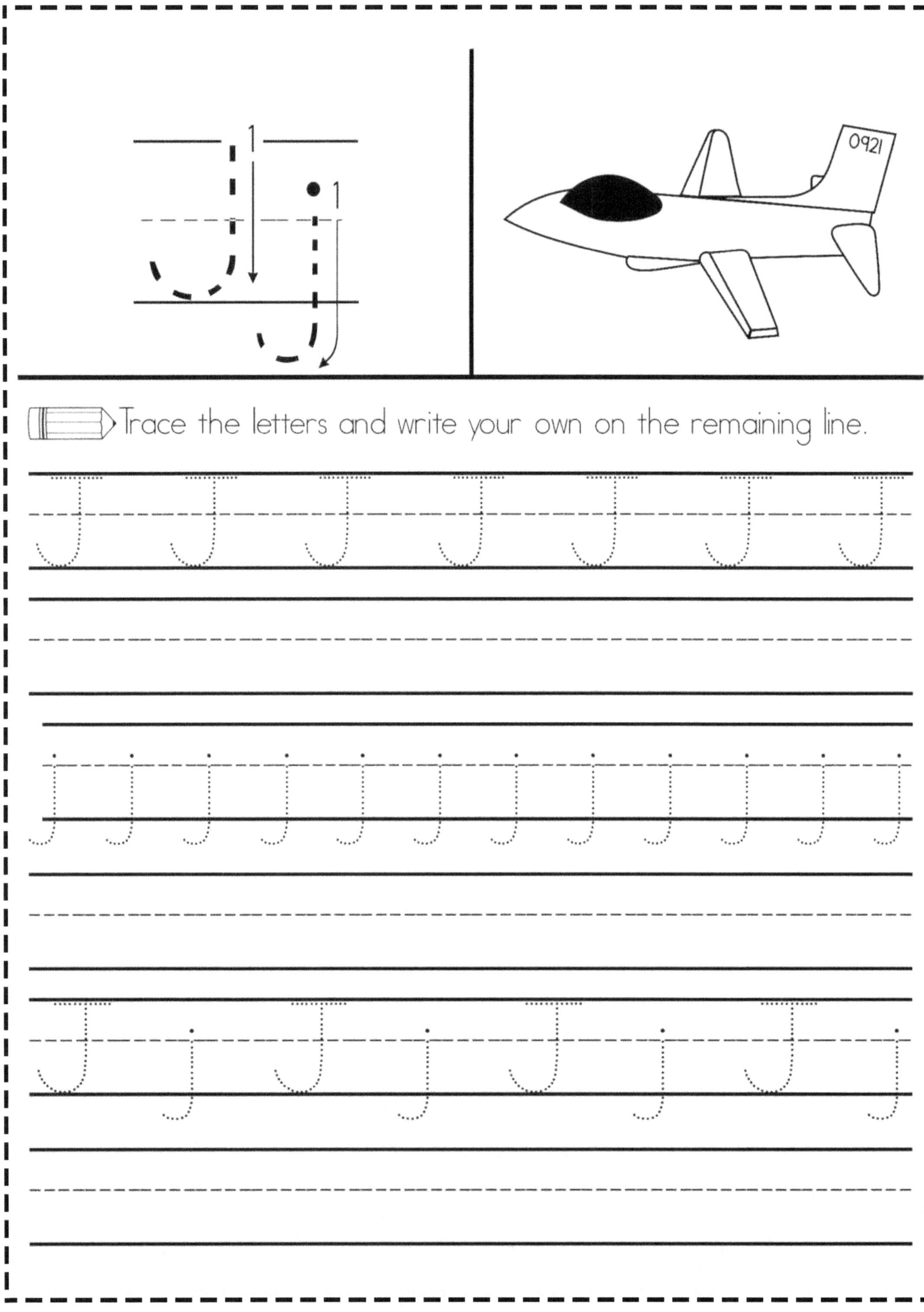

1
1
0921
Trace the letters and write your own on the remaining line.

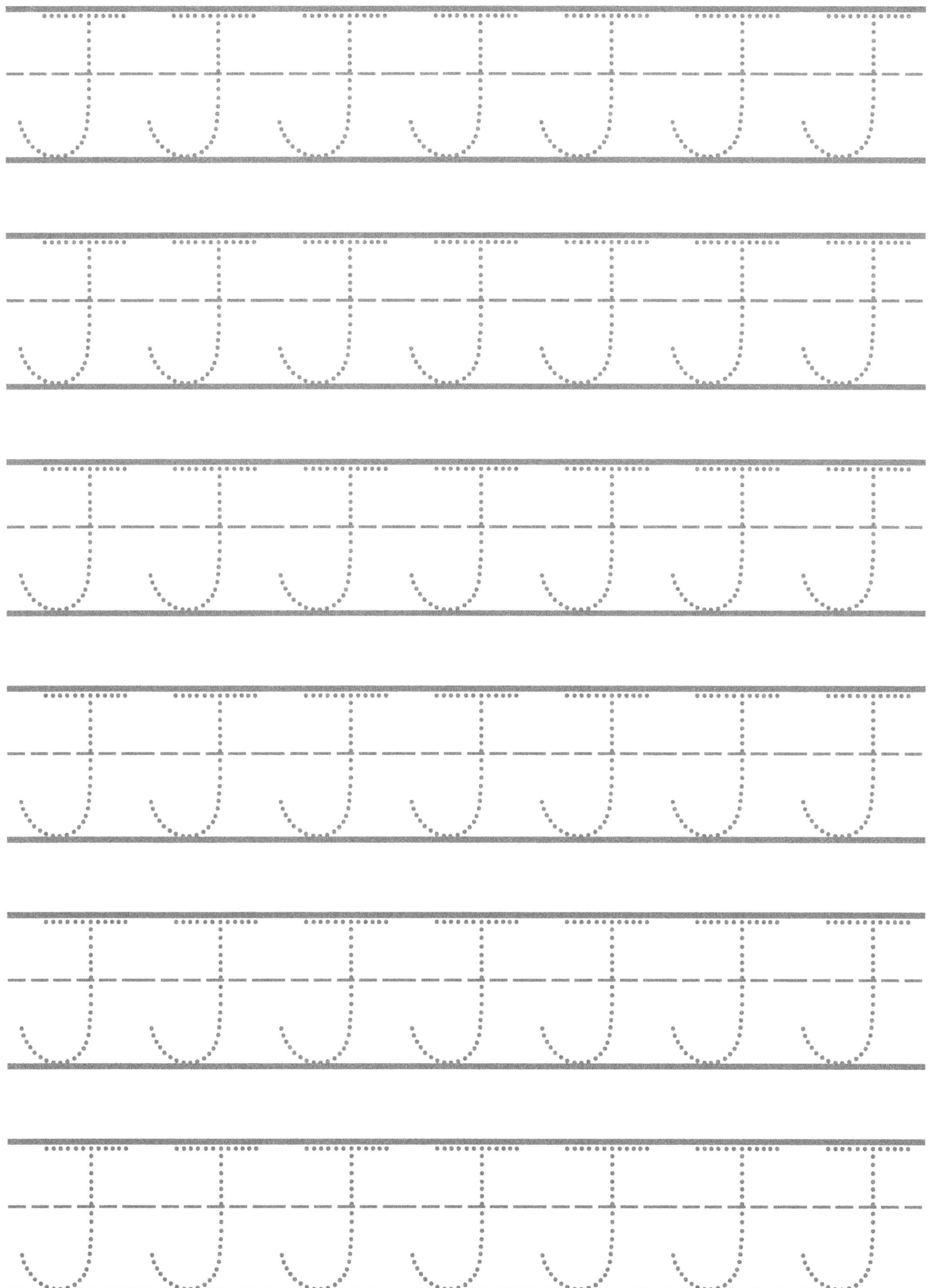

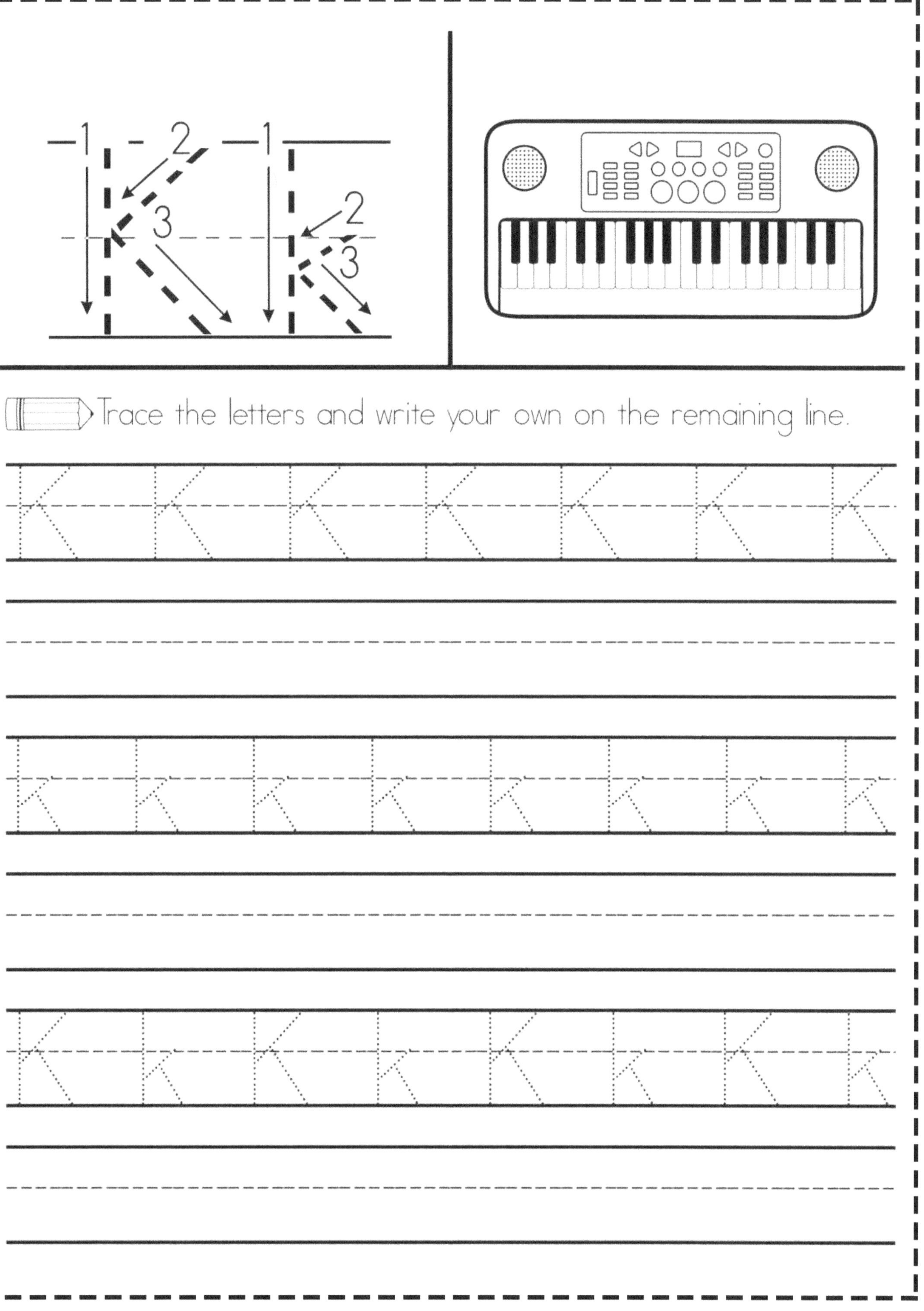

Trace the letters and write your own on the remaining line.

Trace the letters and write your own on the remaining line.

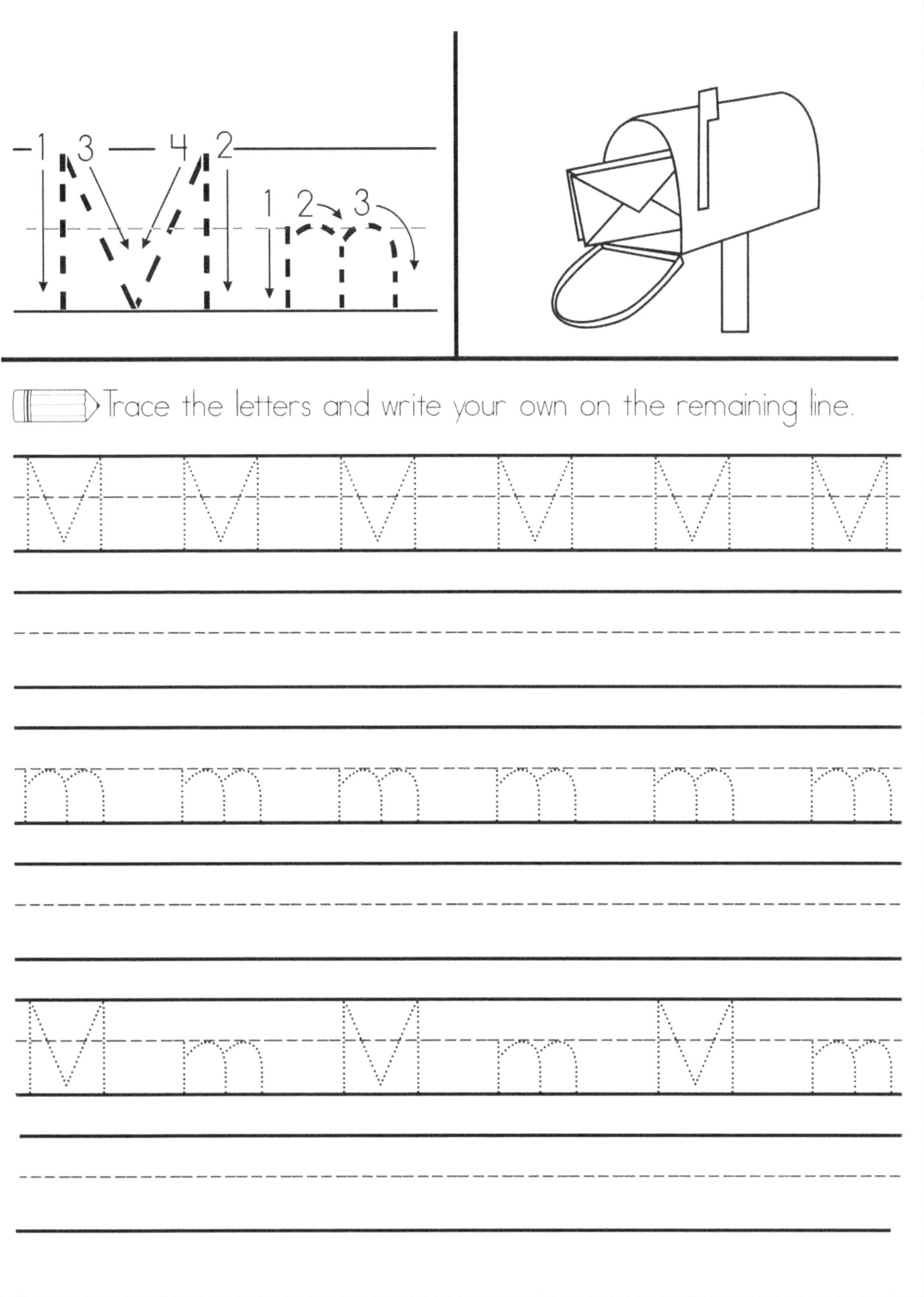

Trace the letters and write your own on the remaining line.

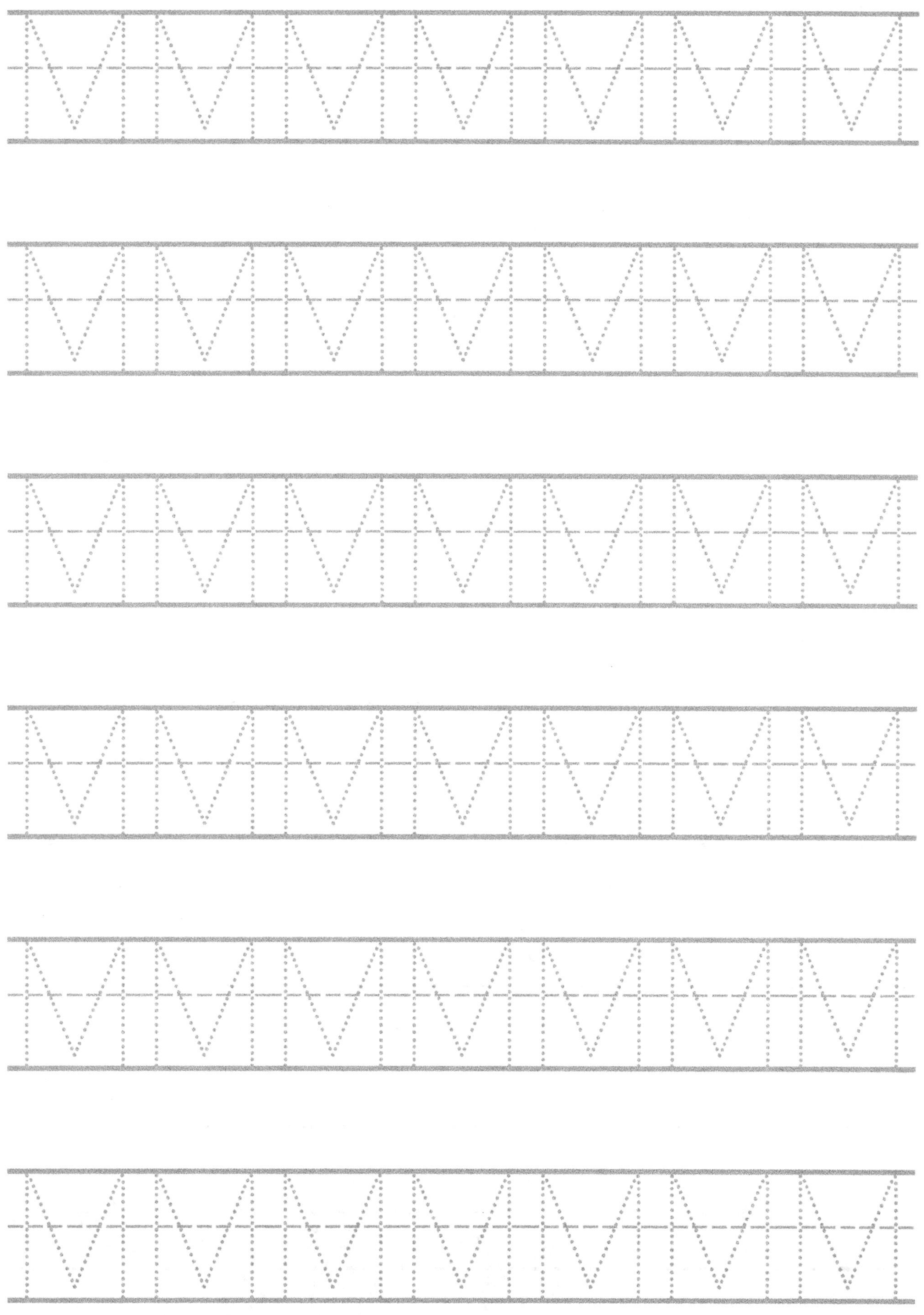

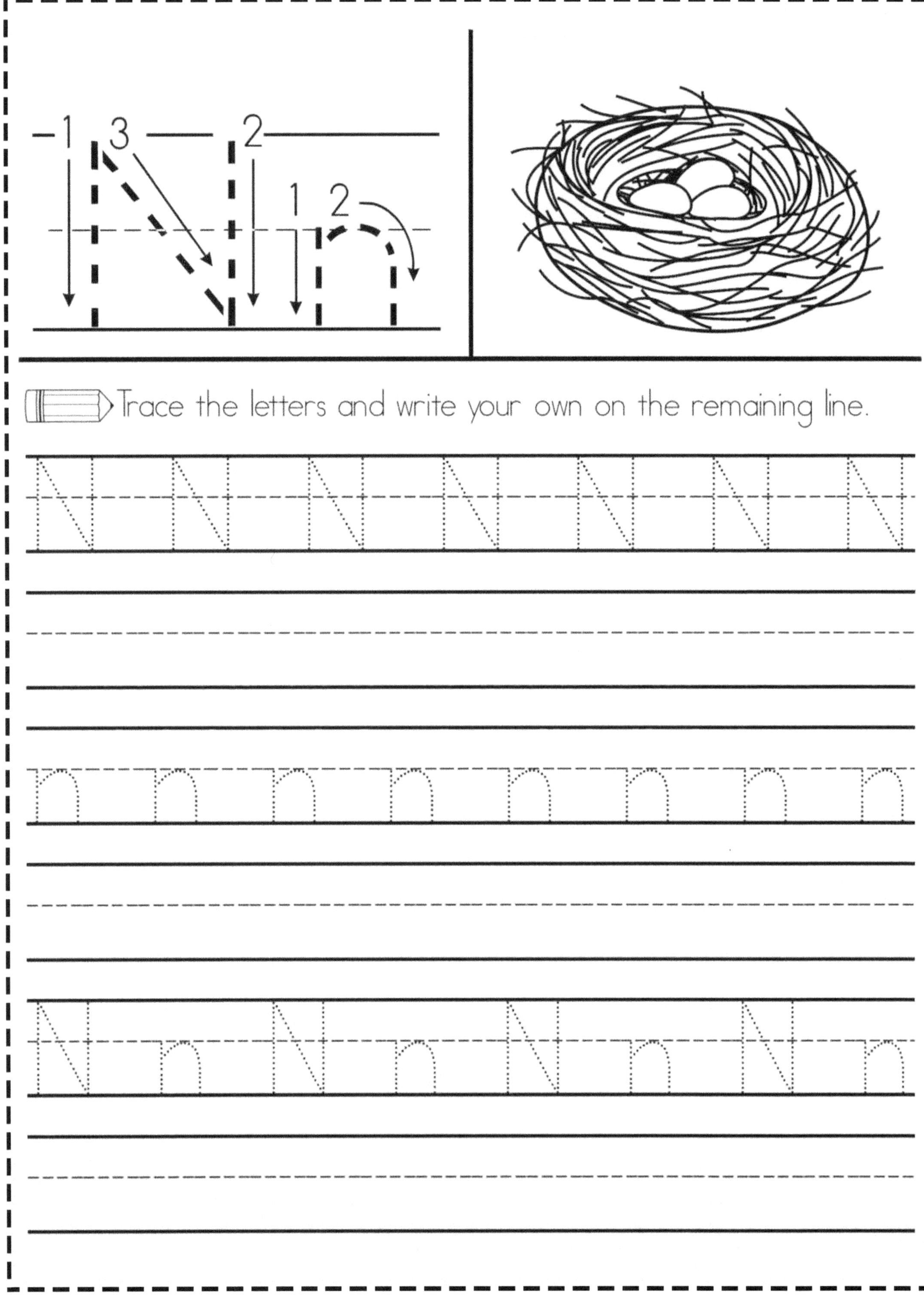

Trace the letters and write your own on the remaining line.

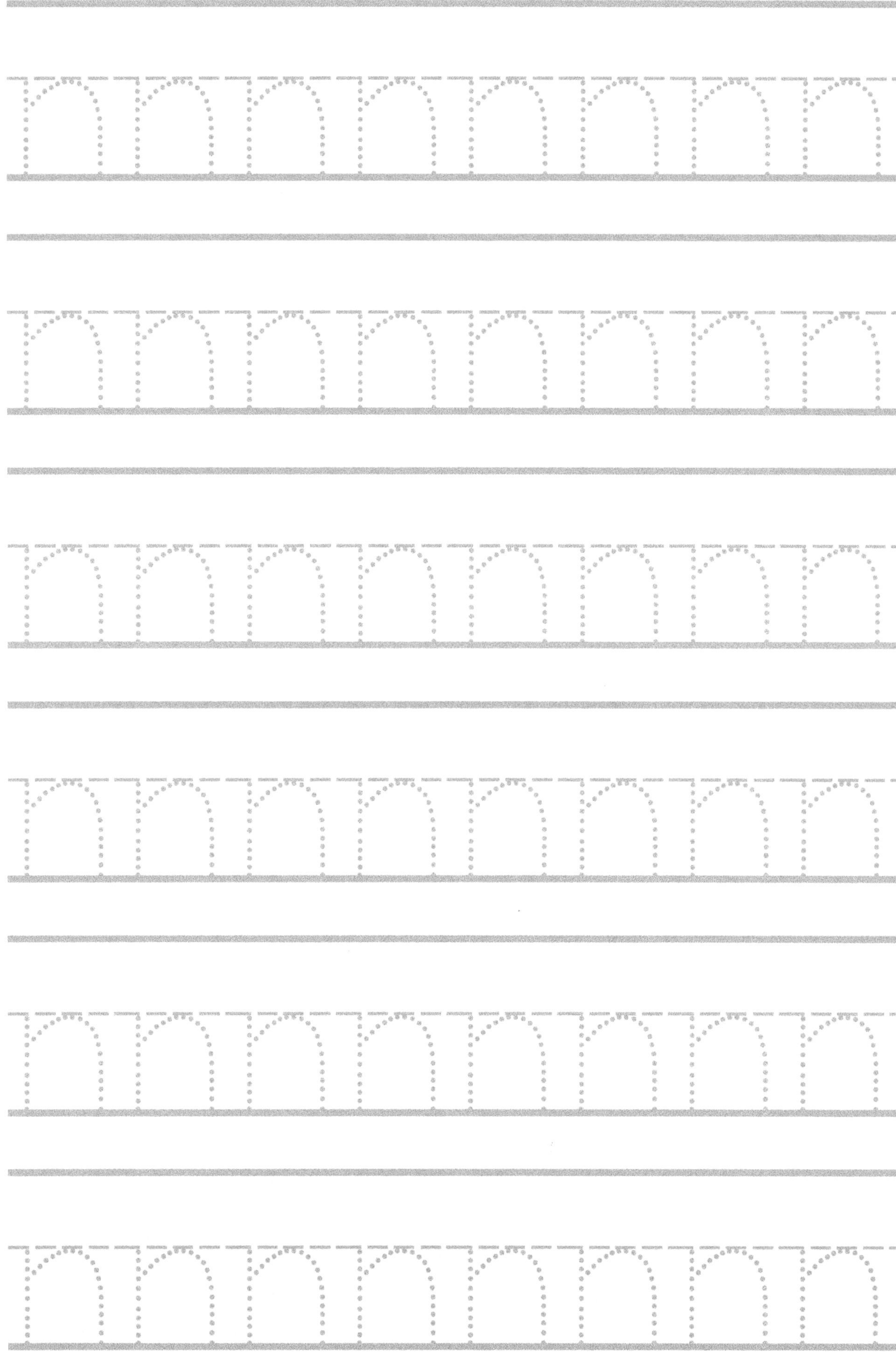

Trace the letters and write your own on the remaining line.

Trace the letters and write your own on the remaining line.

p p p p p p p

p p p p p p

p p p p p p

p p p p p p

p p p p p p

p p p p p p

p p p p p p

p p p p p p

1
1 2
2
Trace the letters and write your own on the remaining line.

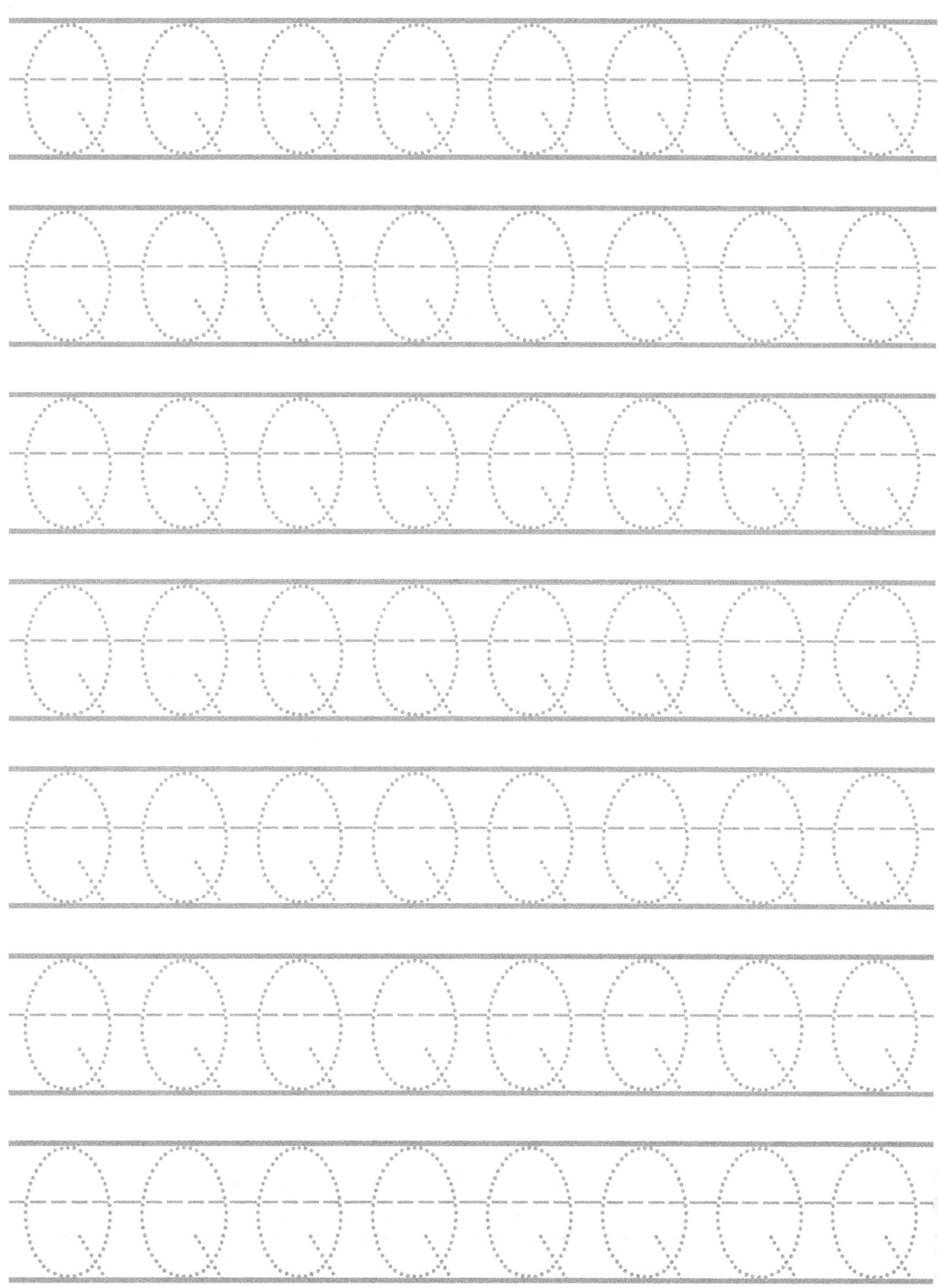

Trace the letters and write your own on the remaining line.

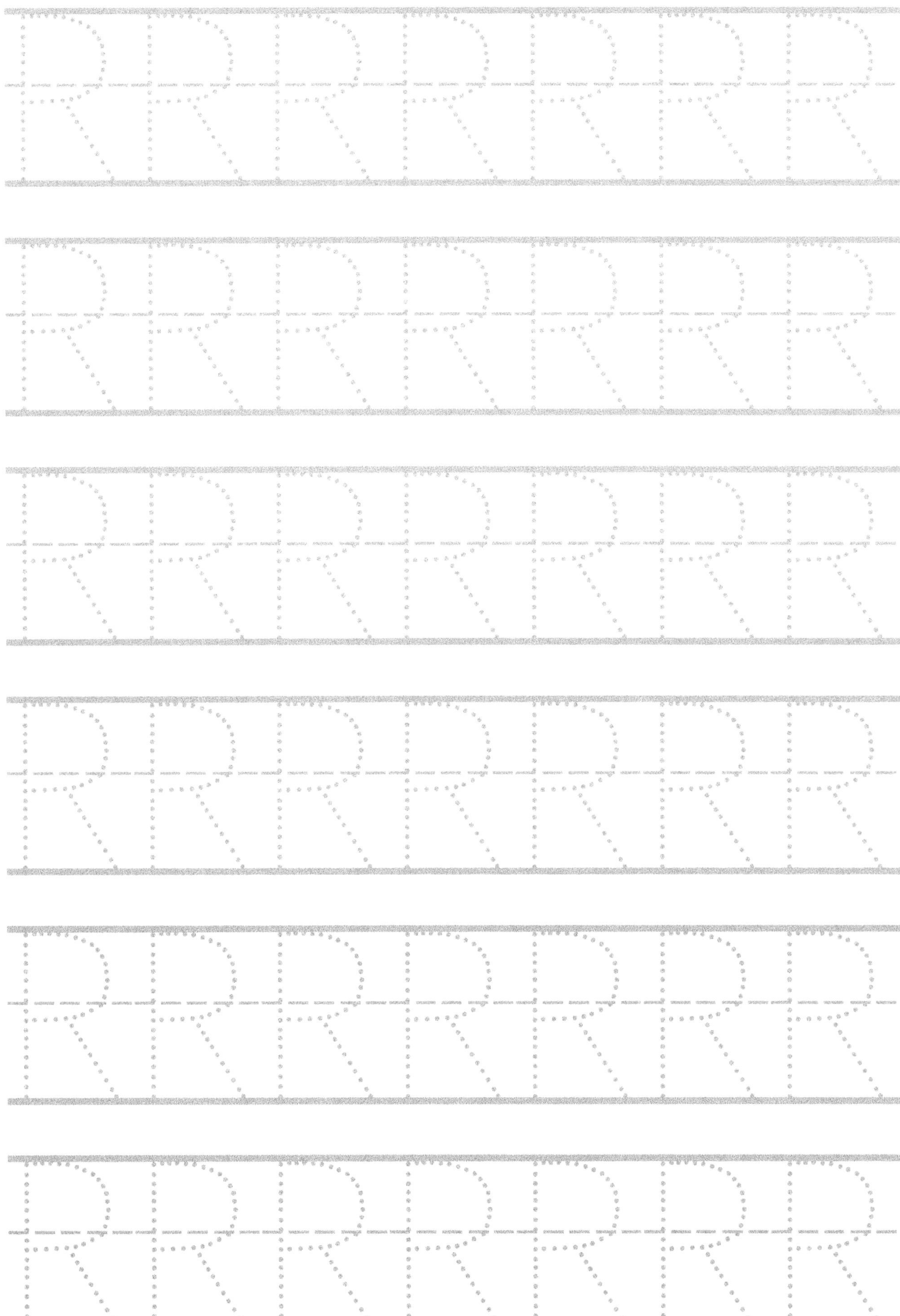

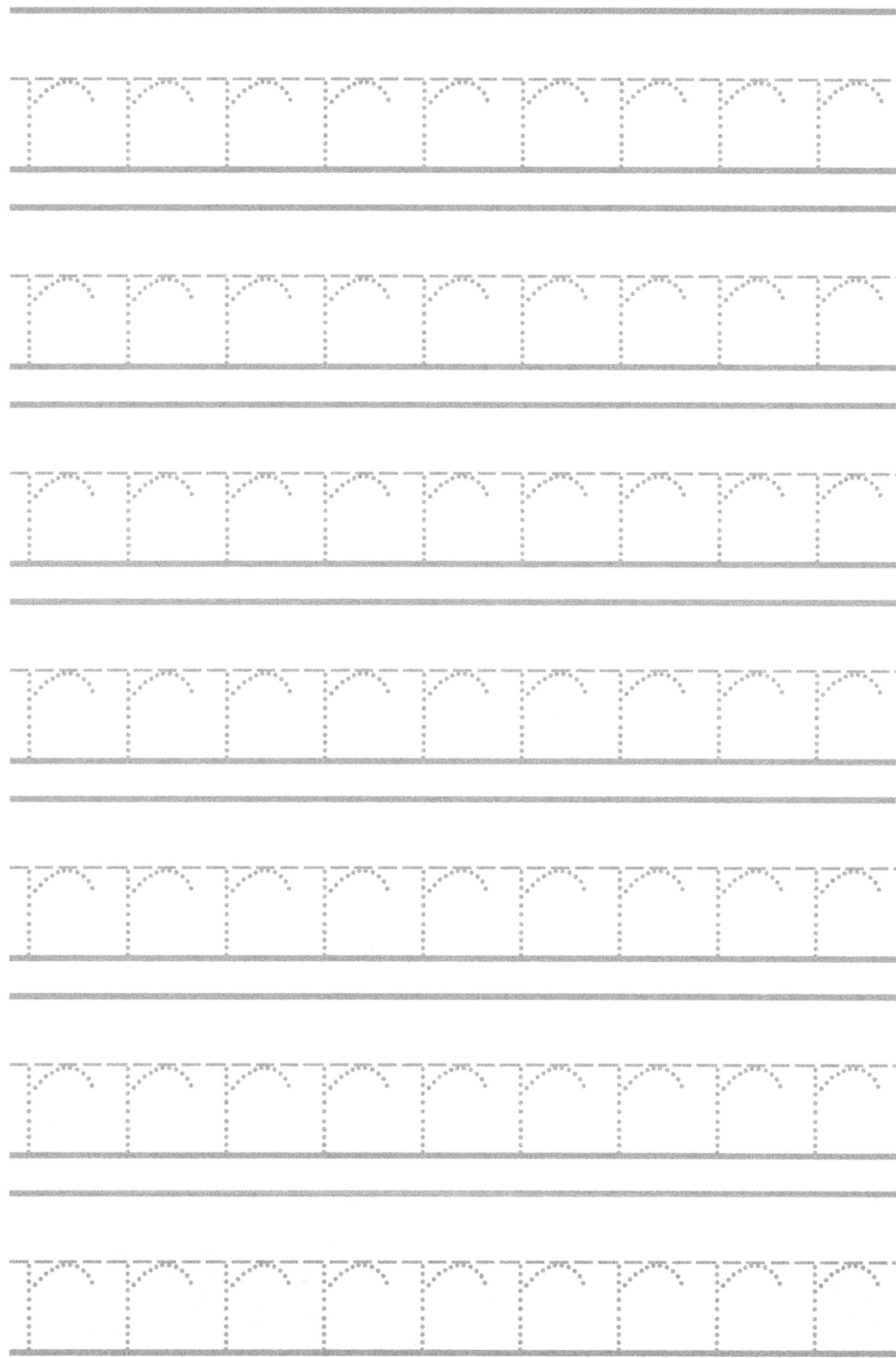

Trace the letters and write your own on the remaining line.

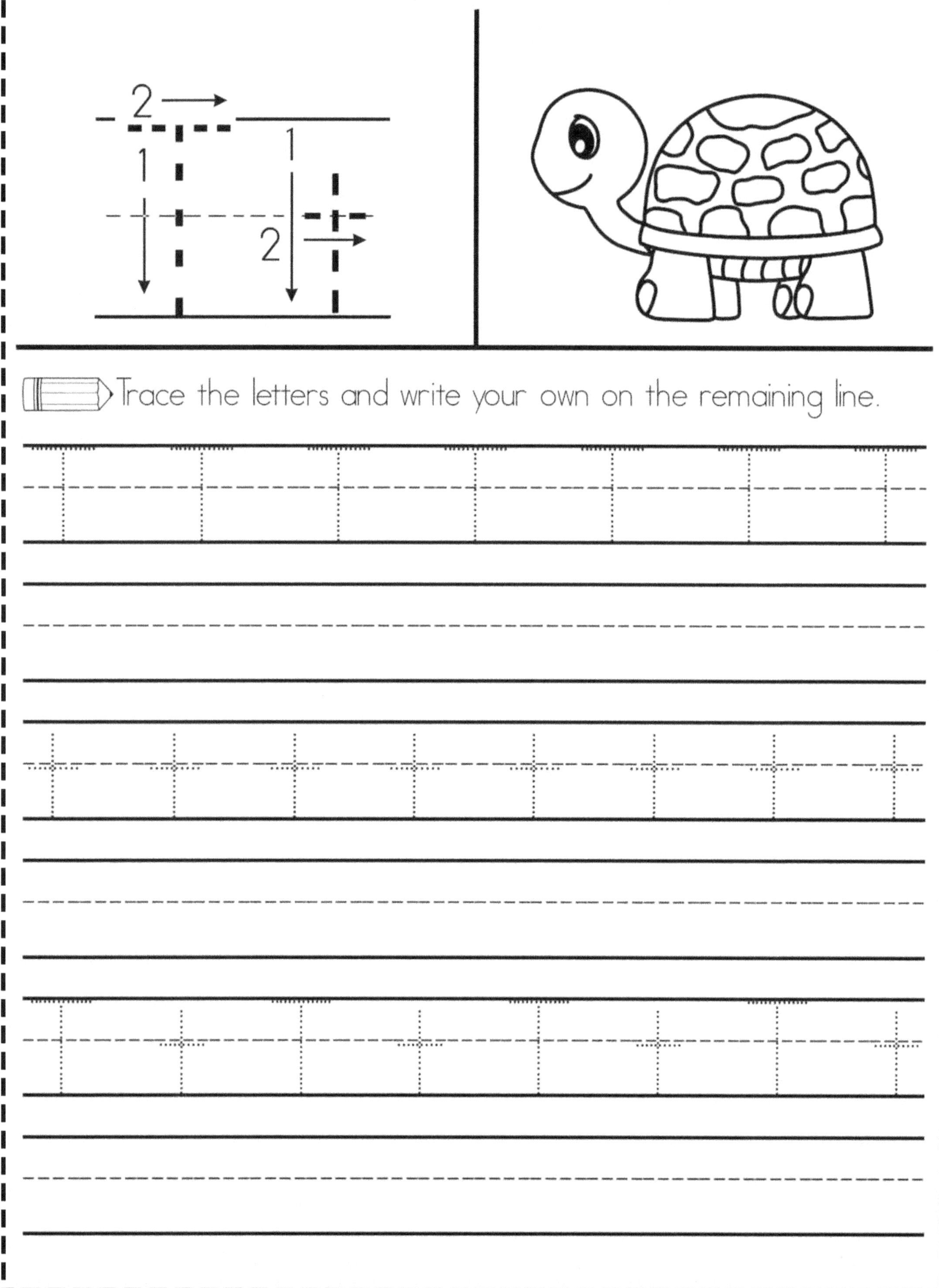

Trace the letters and write your own on the remaining line.

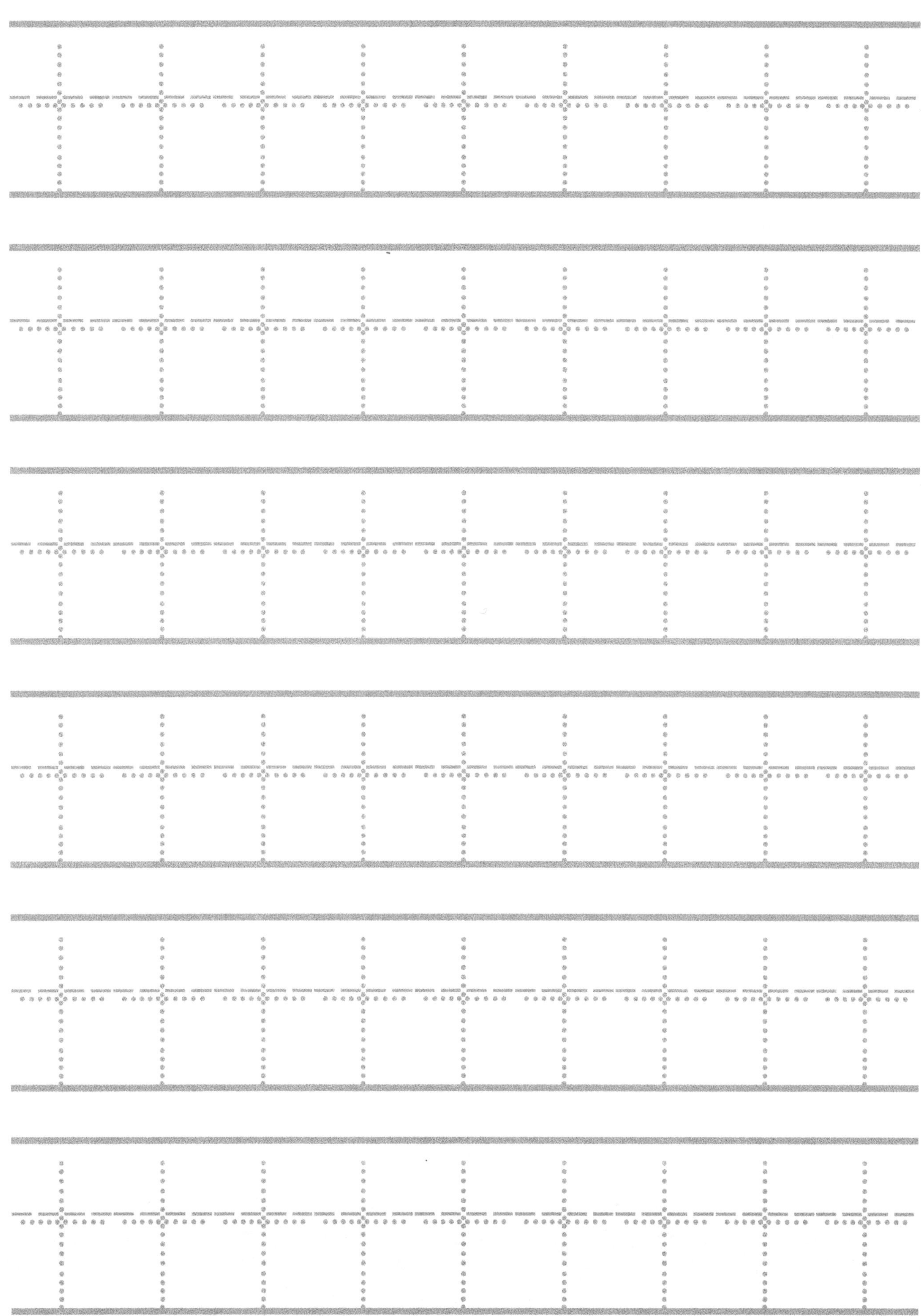

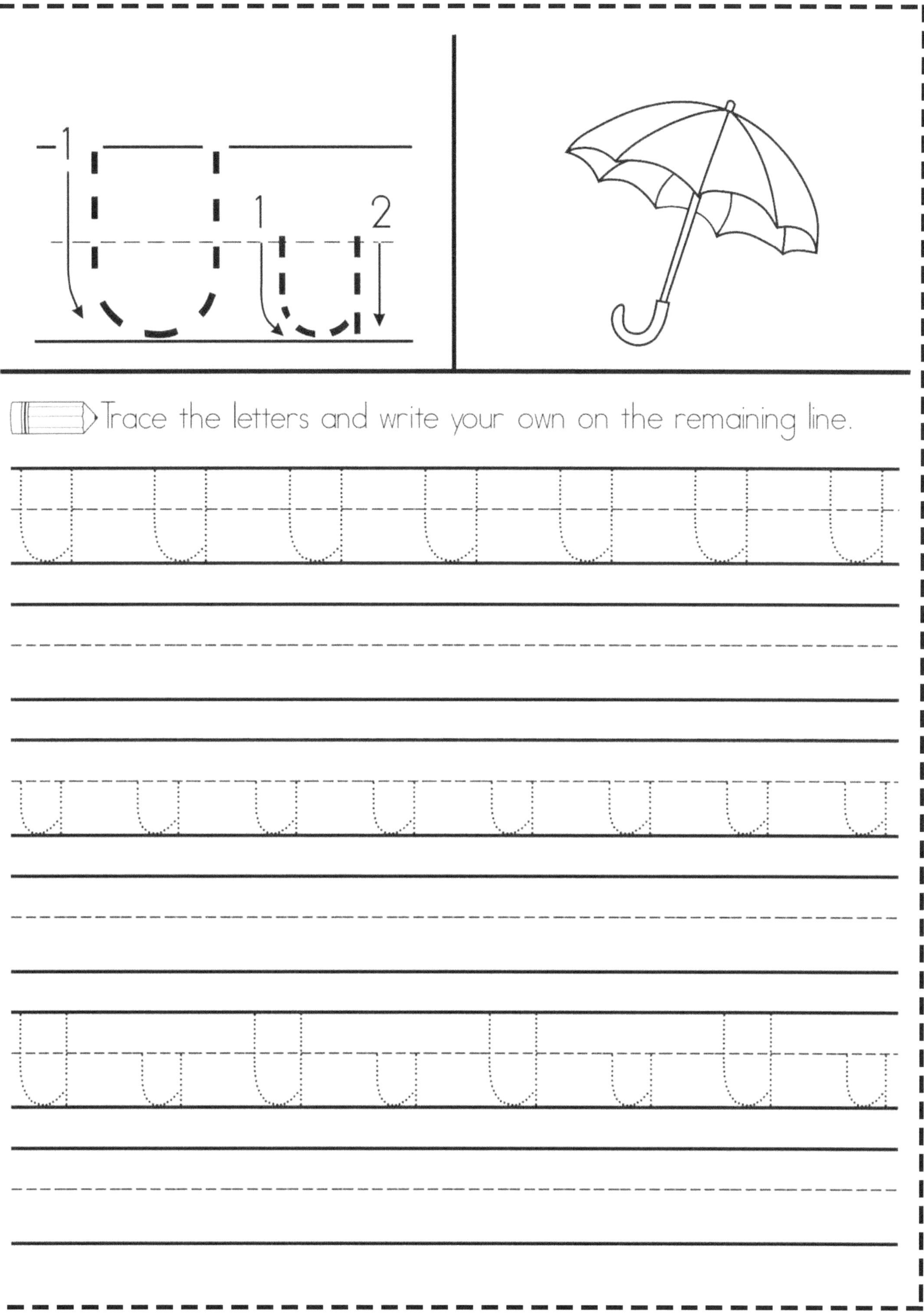

Trace the letters and write your own on the remaining line.

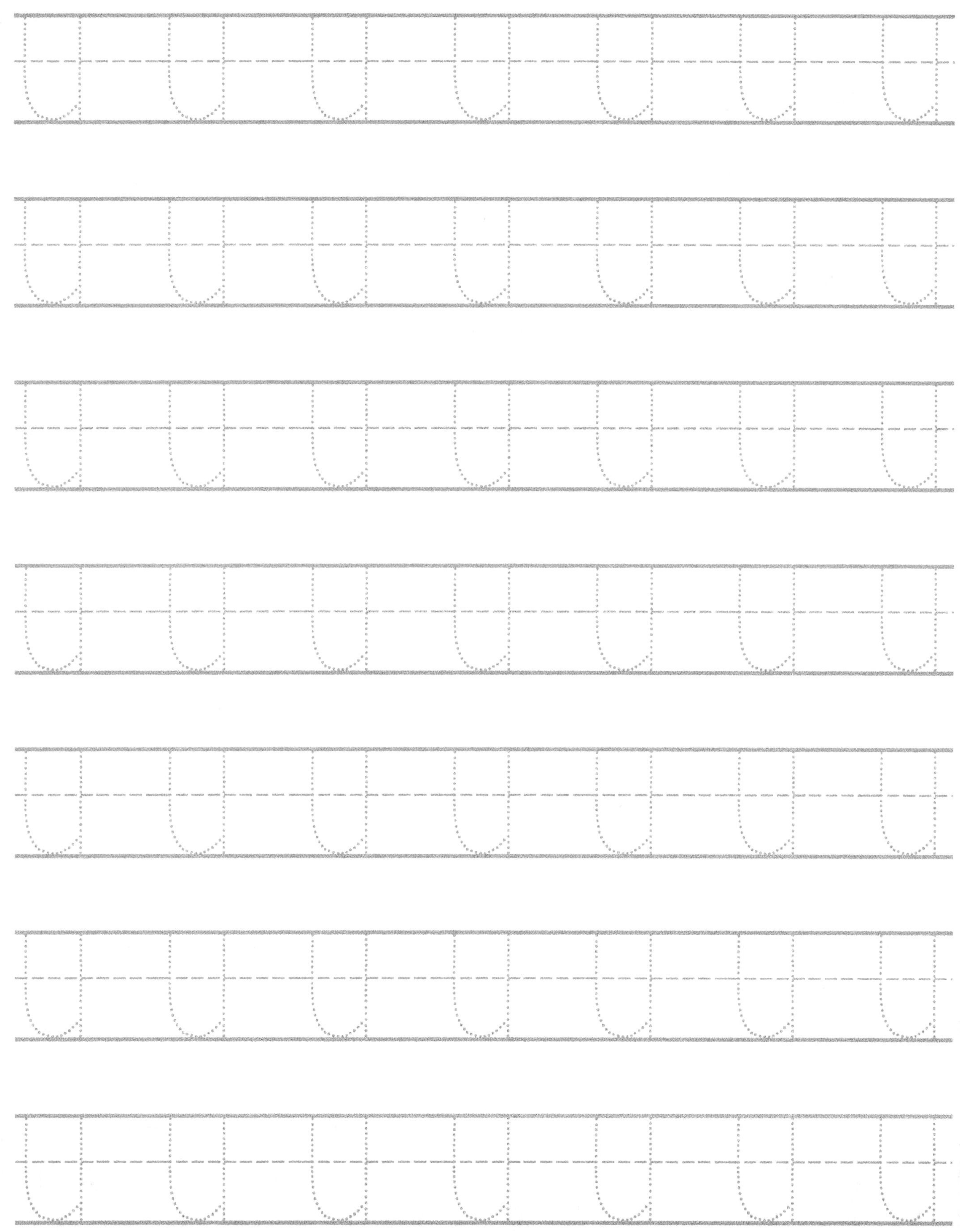

Trace the letters and write your own on the remaining line.

Trace the letters and write your own on the remaining line.

Trace the letters and write your own on the remaining line.

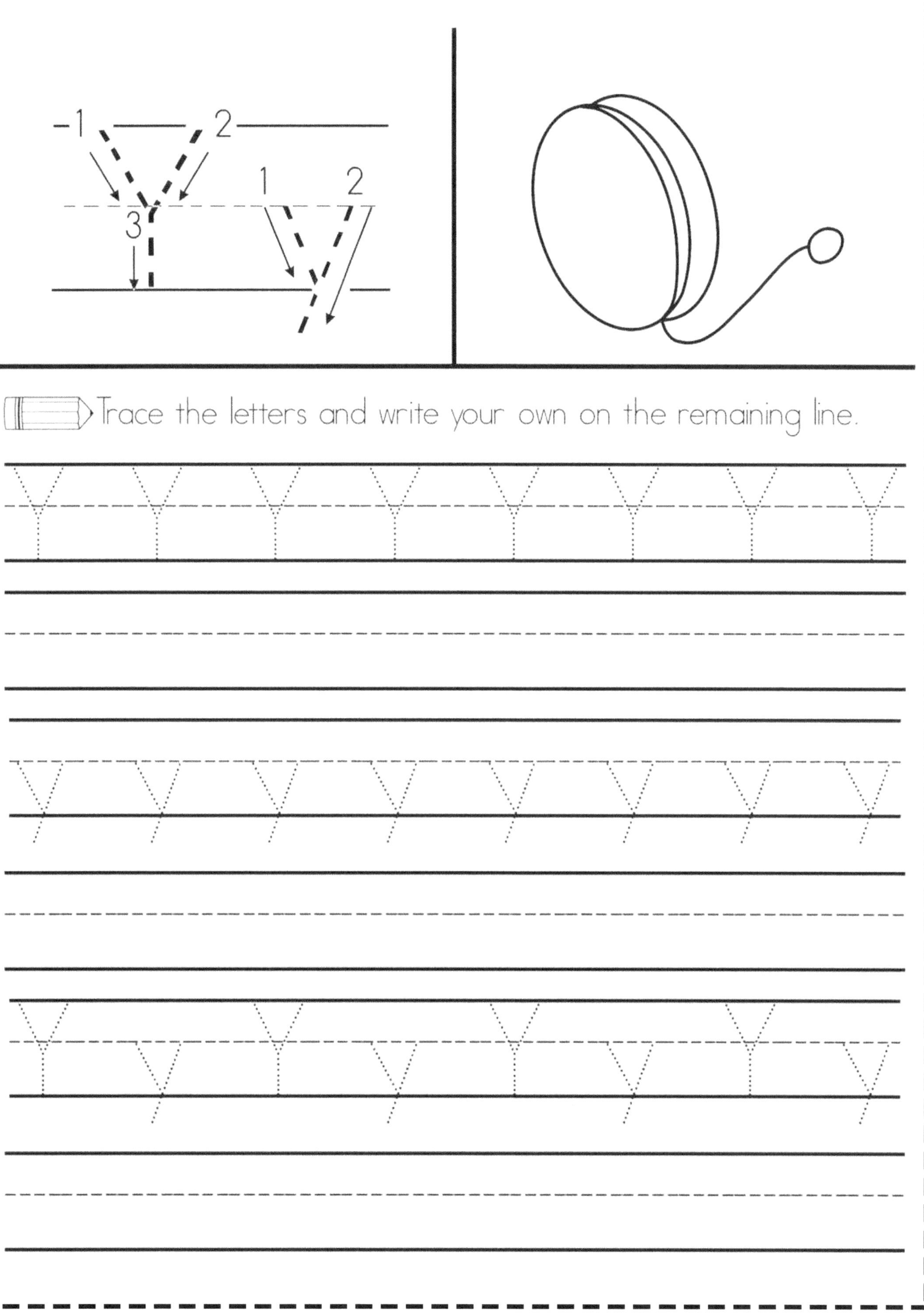

Trace the letters and write your own on the remaining line.

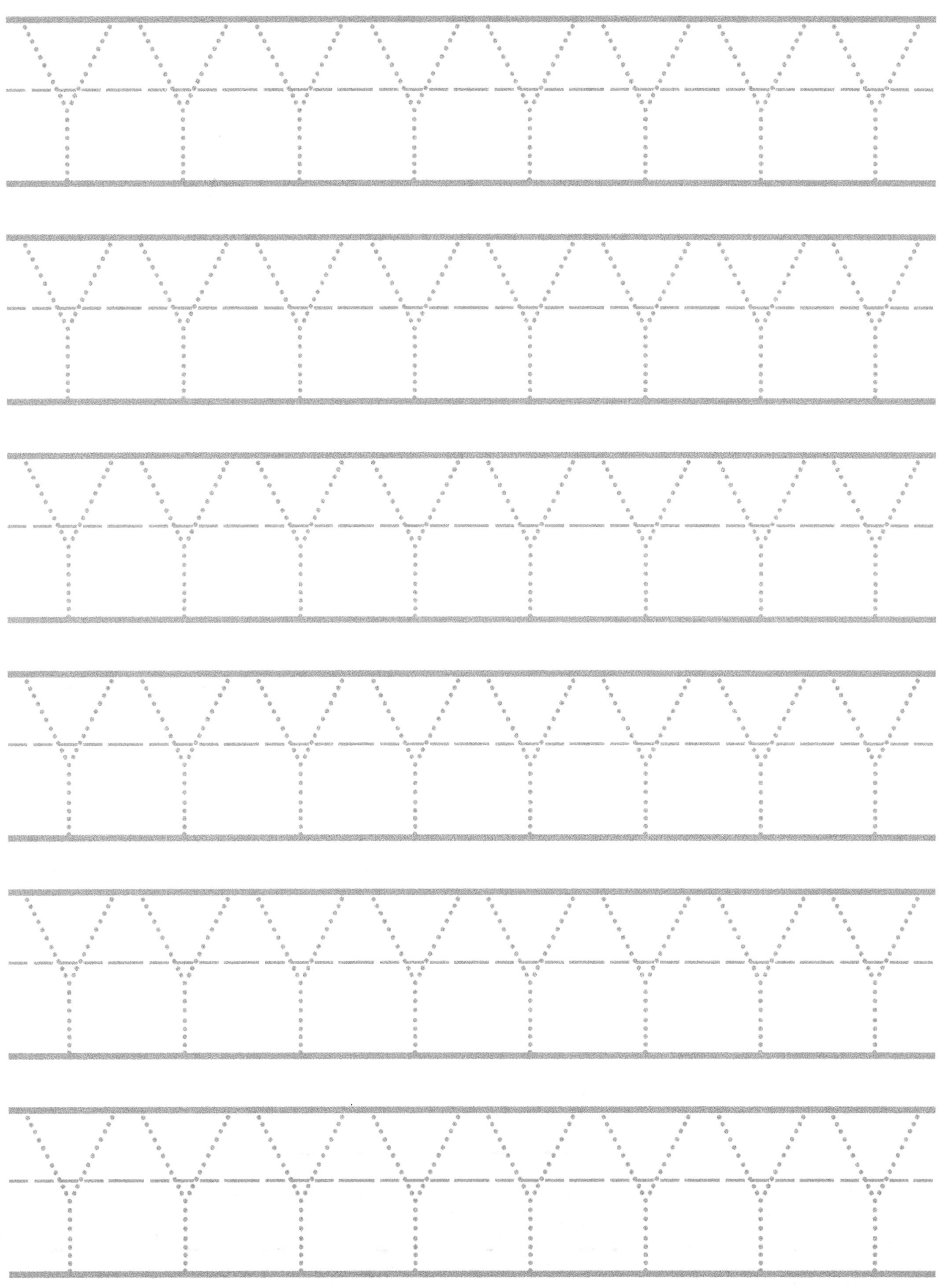

Trace the letters and write your own on the remaining line.